I0116166

Developing 20/20 Foresight

Learning how to have it go your way.

by Sharon W. Doty

Arpeggias, LLC
3061 Northbrook Drive
Atlanta, GA 30341
swdarpeggias@gmail.com
http://www.keepingthemsafe.net

© 2007-2025 by Arpeggias, LLC
Formerly MMDK Consulting, LLC

ISBNs: 978-0-9770953-1-5, 0-9770953-1-2

Library of Congress Cataloging-in-Publication Data
Library of Congress Control Number:
2007920096

DEDICATION

For most of my life, I have been a big sister to someone and Daddy's "little girl." It was my privilege to grow up the oldest and the only girl in a family of six children. One thing my parents taught me was that being a woman did not define me or limit what I was capable of in life.

They said that we could be anything we wanted to be and do anything we wanted to do if we worked hard, respected ourselves and others, and remembered always that family comes first.

No one believed in us more and no one challenged us to go beyond the boxes that society might try to impose on us more than our parents. Of all the gifts that my mother gave me, the gift of knowing myself as capable beyond limitation and the awareness that part of my job in life is to make a difference for others are lessons that impact my life on a daily basis.

Daddy expected nothing but my best and always loved me even when my best was hidden from view. He knew me better than I knew myself. He nurtured my intellect and challenged my thinking. He taught me what it is to love unconditionally and, at the same time, let something grow and make its own way.

This book is my gift to them and I know that they are together again watching down on us and smiling proudly at all that we are.

Thanks, Mom and Dad. As I look around this crazy, loving, kooky, and wonderful family there is only one thing to say. You did good!

ACKNOWLEDGEMENT

There are many people who contributed to the completion of this project. It is not possible to publish this book without acknowledging their participation, their persistence, and their commitment to support me in this project.

To Leslie Zieren for inviting me to do the Landmark Forum in 1996, thanks for seeing something in me that I could not see in myself. Landmark's courses have provided me with the tools I needed to turn dreams and visions into reality.

Thanks to Tomme Fent for saying "yes" when I asked her to work with me on this project. She took it on when the book was only an idea and her weekly calls with me to hold me to account for what I was accomplishing and to keep me in action was the structure that I needed to get the job done. She listened, she demanded, she edited, and she challenged and this book is the result.

For all those I interviewed for the book. Thanks for saying "yes" without knowing what you were getting into. You took on the project as if it were your own. It was your willingness to look for answers to questions you had not previously considered that made the book possible.

To my husband Ned, who was the wind beneath my wings for almost 45 years — your love and trust gave me the courage to live my dreams and to keep living forever and always.

Sharon Womack Doty

FOREWORD...

Do you consider yourself to be a "mission driven" or "mission oriented" individual? Do others characterize you as a "high achiever" who is self-motivated? Do you commit yourself to continual self-improvement and personal growth?
Then you will find this book to be of value.

Perhaps you are well intentioned but dissatisfied with your apparent inability to accomplish your mission, to achieve your goals, to develop your desired skills.
Then you will find this book to be of value.

Maybe you fit someplace "in between" these states of being – generally capable, typically competent, usually satisfied with the results you obtain in your life pursuits – but nonetheless, confident that you could, and should, be doing better.
Then you will find this book to be of value.

The fact is that the author has done an excellent job of creating a very straight–forward, common sense, easily accessible process that anyone can employ to further develop her/his proficiency in any endeavor. Her 20/20 Foresight process establishes a framework or roadmap that every person can use to improve her/his performance. It does this by clearly delineating and defining the actual steps – and the order of these steps – consistently employed by successful people to attain expertise that eventually is of such a high order that it produces positive results almost "automatically" or as "second nature."

She identified this framework and process via research conducted with a very diverse and disparate group of people who did have at least one thing in common – highly honed and refined expertise that they each continually utilize to produce things of value – in their own lives and for others around them.

The author's desire was that all people would have access to the same sort of tools/skills that her

4

"expert" group possessed, so that they could employ these tools/skills to enrich their lives; the lives of their family and friends; and even the lives of all those in the broader community around them.

Her solution was to identify these tools/skills, to isolate their order of application, to explain the use of each one and then to assemble them into a truly valuable and easy to use framework and related process – 20/20 Foresight.

You will find this book filled with interesting background information derived from the lives of both the author, and also, her "expert" group. Finally, to "put the icing on the cake," this book is a quick read and very accessible, but nevertheless a valuable resource for future reference whenever you wish to "polish" your facility with 20/20 Foresight.

Michael J. Bemi
Lisle, Illinois

What participants say...

"I completely shifted the way I view developing mastery from something difficult and only available to certain kinds of people to a specific process that I was already proficient with. We've all mastered something. I recommend this book to anyone who wants to master anything in life."

SHANNON WIMBERLY

"What a concept! To actually get present enough to identify and distinguish each of the steps to becoming masterful... I had never considered HOW I became proficient performing certain tasks, while completely bumbling others. I have a greater understanding of how my early choices and passions have become my current vocations and avocations. This is a must read for anyone committed to being a master! Thanks for the opportunity to participate!"

CATHY TUTTY

"This book advances an exciting new approach to learning and becoming proficient in any area of one's choosing. This learning method has practical application to an overwhelmingly wide range of interests. I highly recommend this book to anyone who has a desire to build expertise in any area of interest."

TOMME FENT

"Being selected and questioned was a rare opportunity. Often in life we do not look upon our gifts as being gifts, and they go unnoticed or overlooked because all we see is the things we cannot do. We each have rare and unique gifts/talents, this inquiry let me see that."

BRIAN WIMBERLY

CHAPTER ONE

What is 20/20 Foresight?

At approximately 3:00 a.m. on December 1, 2001, a firebug with a particular fondness for red cars set fire to my husband's red Ford F150 pickup and my red Grand Marquis in the driveway of our house. When it was all over, there was nothing much left of the front end of either car.

As we were dealing with the mess, the trauma, and the inconvenience of needing to shop for and buy new cars, our oldest daughter suggested to me that I finally buy the car I really wanted. Over the years, I had purchased cars based on need, practicality, and what I thought I could have or afford but they were never the one I really wanted, the car I dreamed about. So, I decided to ask my car dealer for what I wanted and a couple of hours later, I drove my dream car, a 2002 Lincoln Town Car Executive Series, off the lot. It was and is very special to me.

A few weeks later, I was entering the expressway at an on-ramp that is both an entrance to the expressway and the next exit off the same road. It is also on the downside of a hill. In my side view mirror I noticed a car in the right-hand lane coming over the hill a little fast. In addition to the fact that the driver was speeding, the car was dented up and it looked like the dents had been hammered out from the inside of the car.

All my internal warning signs went off at the same time and I began to watch the car and driver carefully because I had a feeling that the driver was going to do something dangerous or threatening.

As it happens, the car pulled in front of me suddenly, without warning or any kind of signal, to get off the expressway at the next exit in the same lane where I was getting on the highway. If I had not been paying attention and had not noticed the signs that warned me of impending disaster, my dream car and I probably would have parted company just as we were beginning to get acquainted.

This is just one example of the kind of thing that happens day after day on the highways and byways of our country. Every day, millions of people drive big, powerful vehicles across roadways that vary in size and condition—and most of those hours and miles are uneventful.[i] If you have been in an accident this year, the facts may be of little consolation but the truth is that, according to the Department of Transportation, 2017 marked a new low in the number of vehicle fatalities for every 100 million vehicle miles driven each day in the United States—only 1.06[ii].

Obviously, this low number is not insignificant to those families who lost loved ones because of an automobile accident. However, it seems as though an adult is much more likely to die of a number of other causes than to be killed in a car accident.

It is also true that the youngest and most inexperienced drivers, those between the ages of 16 and 25, had the highest rate of involvement in crashes that included fatalities.[iii]

So, for those of us over 25, the probability that we will be involved in a fatal automobile accident is fairly low. Why is that? It is not just that we know how to drive a car. Knowing something works or doesn't work or knowing how to make something better rarely makes a difference. Even when we know that all we need to do is change the way we do something to make a situation better and stop things from going the way they have always gone before, we don't always do what we need to do to make changes.

We see examples of this around us every day. Lots of research studies show that even when we know how to reduce the likelihood that we will die by changing some of our behaviors, we don't do it. Knowing that something is bad for us or knowing what we need to do to be healthier does not seem to have much impact on whether we change our behavior.

In fact, the way we deal with our fitness issues is a good illustration of how "knowing" doesn't really provide much of anything. If you ask any group of people whether they know how to eat properly and what to do to be fit, the answer is "yes." We know how to eat better and get more exercise and we know these things will help prevent heart attacks and reduce the risk of stroke, but all we have to do is look around to see that this country is overweight and out of shape. Knowing that we need to lose weight and exercise more in order to live longer is making no difference.[iv] In fact, when it comes to our health and fitness, it sometimes seems that for most of us, the older we get the more likely we are to gain weight and exercise less.

So why is driving different? Why do drivers over the age of 25 have fewer fatal accidents? Why is it that the longer we drive, the better we get at avoiding accidents and driving safely?

Perhaps driving is different because while we learned to drive, we also developed something I call 20/20 Foresight in that particular area of our lives.

20/20 Foresight

Everyone knows about 20/20 hindsight. It is perfect! We look back over our shoulder at the past or we think about what happened and have no trouble seeing what we should have or could have done differently in a situation. We see where we made mistakes or where we simply went the wrong way. Our view from that vantage point is clear and unspoiled.

Unfortunately, we can't see into the future in the same way. We can't see the future with the same kind of clarity and precision—or can we? What do we mean by *20/20 Foresight*, and how has having it or using it made us safer drivers?

Obviously, *20/20 Foresight* is about more than simply knowing what to do. If knowing or having knowledge was all that was needed, younger drivers would be as safe on the road as those of us who are over 25. After all, they are the ones who have studied the manuals and demonstrated their knowledge by passing both a written test and a driving test.

Of course, there are things we all need to *know* about driving in order to drive safely on the highway. Drivers need to know how to operate a car and how to drive it. They need to know the rules of the road and much, much more. So, while knowledge is obviously a necessary element, knowing is not enough to increase our safety on the road.

The question then becomes, "If *20/20 Foresight* is not about how much we know and it is not about having a crystal ball or some other method of seeing into the future, what is it?"

Simply put, *20/20 Foresight* is a level of competence and know-how that includes two specific elements: 1) a high level of expertise, and 2) the ability to identify potentially risky situations or circumstances before they happen and take action to avoid disaster or prevent mistakes. *20/20 Foresight* is the ability, in certain areas of our life, to see the world in such a way that we can anticipate what is probably going to happen next—positive and negative—and when we see potential risks, we react automatically to steer clear of approaching problems or challenges.

Often, when we think about being proficient or having expertise in a particular area of life, we think about such things as being good at our job or a hobby or sport. Sometimes we simply think we have done something so often or learned it so well that it has become second nature to us. Maybe there is more to this than just knowing things or repeating something so often that it becomes a kind of habit. Perhaps there is something more at work here than we have thought about before—and maybe, if we can figure out what that "something more" is, we can apply it to other areas of our life.

Wouldn't it be great to have the tools to bring the same level of expertise to other areas of life that we bring to driving or to our job or favorite hobby? *Developing 20/20 Foresight* is an attempt to examine this prospect and see whether identifying the steps in the process of becoming proficient provides us with any access to applying the tools to other areas of our life.

To begin to get an idea of what it means to develop *20/20 Foresight*, let's look again at our experience of driving a car—starting at the beginning. Remember the first time you got behind the wheel of a car to drive on the highway in traffic? For most of us, the experience followed weeks of reading manuals and practicing driving back and forth in the driveway or around the block where we lived. Some had the opportunity to practice maneuvering a car through fields and over meadows on the farm or on country roads. But now we were venturing out into the real world. We were going to drive on the road with other cars. The experience was both exhilarating and terrifying. This was our first real taste of freedom and our first realization that this was a big responsibility and a little (or a lot) scary.

Excitement, arrogance, and self-assurance were sufficient to sustain us as we backed out of the driveway and headed into oncoming traffic. At that moment, however, we realized that no matter how cool we wanted others to think we were, this was as terrifying as it was exciting. We got a death grip on the steering wheel because it seemed as if every car was headed straight for us. Those traveling toward us looked like they were crossing the centerline to hit us head-on, and those beside us were surely inching over into our lane and about to run us off the road.

Over time, with practice, we realized that our initial fears were unfounded. Experience taught us that there were parameters or boundaries for *normal* behavior from other drivers on the road, and as long as we watch for the signs and notice when someone crosses the line, we can travel safely.

As a result, we developed *20/20 Foresight* when it comes to driving. This means most of the time, we see the signs of a potential danger and take appropriate actions to avoid the problem. Think about the number of times we realize that we have just avoided an accident— the number of times we've had a "near miss" on the highway. It was these situations and circumstances that provoked exploration of this phenomenon of *20/20 Foresight*.

Driving is not the only example of our ability to develop proficiencies and demonstrate an ability to see the warning signs of impending, potentially harmful consequences. These proficiencies allow us to intervene and prevent many unfortunate situations from occurring—large and small.

Pilots look ahead to see possible challenges in the weather before they even take off, and as they fly, they watch for other possible risks that might appear in the sky. This ability is the same one that is there for a dressmaker who is cutting out a pattern and fitting a new design. In fact, many people have this same level of know-how in their work and professional life as well as with hobbies and leisure activities. In these areas, people have developed some expertise—some level of ability—that is in the back of their mind and through which they see their activities. This filter, of sorts, allows them to sort out and recognize the warning signs that something is about to go wrong and, most of the time, they are able to take appropriate action to interrupt the flow and avoid any harm.

Although most of us have the ability to call on this expertise in specific areas of our life, we seem to think that is just the way we do things, and so we take it for granted.

However, what if this ability **is** derived from a set of skills that are a natural part of how human beings operate? What if human beings could identify and further develop these skills so as to rely on them to develop competencies in other areas? What if identifying and developing these skills could enhance our ability to complete projects, learn new things, or follow through with resolutions and goals? Perhaps by identifying these skills and honing this ability that we have taken for granted until now, we can begin to accomplish new objectives and develop new proficiencies.

CHAPTER TWO

Where did this idea come from?

In 1998, The National Catholic Risk Retention Group, Inc.ᵛ ("TNCRRG") took on the monumental task of developing a child sexual abuse prevention program that focused on educating adults and communities about how to prevent child sexual abuse. The focus of the program was innovative. Up until that time, prevention programming for child sexual abuse centered on teaching children to: "Say 'no,' run away, and tell somebody." Adults were taught how to recognize the signs and symptoms that a child might already have been abused and how to deal with disclosures.

As an expert consultant to the program development team and Chair of the Expert Consulting Team created by TNCRRG, I spent the next four years on a team researching and creating an innovative, cutting-edge program for implementation in the Catholic Church in the United States. The program, *Protecting God's Children™ for Adults* ("PGCA"), was piloted, completed, and ready to roll out to the shareholder dioceses and risk pooling trust of TNCRRG in January 2002, when the Boston Globe published the pivotal article that shined a light on the crisis involving clergy who sexually abused children.

PGCA has three objectives: 1) raise awareness about the nature and scope of the problem of child sexual abuse, 2) provide adults with simple steps to follow to prevent abuse, and 3) provide ongoing training to assure that adults can use the information productively and create safer environments. The program includes elements that address each of the major learning modalities of adults. In addition, it acknowledges that a one-time presentation of innovative material is awareness education—not training.

TNCRRG knew that training was a necessary element for and real practical application of the material in society. Training could best be accomplished through reinforcement of the different aspects of the program over time in smaller pieces. In this way, adults could really use the information provided to recognize the potentially risky behavior of other adults in the environment. *PGCA* training was designed for delivery through the Internet over an extended period of time in short, focused articles.

The original implementation plan was to begin by engaging the bishop and other key leaders in a diocese in the value and importance of the program as a diocesan project. Through them, and with the help of the team of experts who developed the program, a diocese would conduct a campaign to build interest among adults in the diocese and encourage them to participate in the program.

The idea was to let parents, teachers, coaches, youth ministers, and other caring adults know about the problem, and then give them what they needed to train themselves to protect children by becoming skilled at recognizing certain risky behaviors in the adults who are around children and young people and then taking steps to protect the children.

TNCRRG knew that having the participants "buy in" to the program was key to implementing the training elements and achieving the ultimate goal of protecting children and preventing child sexual abuse. Training would require a commitment on the part of participants to further develop their ability to recognize adults whose behavior indicated they were a potential risk to children, and to intervene and interrupt suspicious situations.

As the Catholic Church crisis erupted, the bishops decided that one of the actions they would take was to mandate child sexual abuse awareness training for adults who regularly interact with children across all dioceses. They adopted the *Charter for the Protection of Children and Young People*,[vi] and dioceses across the United States began adopting and implementing safe environment programs in their parishes, schools, and organizations.

Between 2002 and 2020, more than 125 dioceses in the United States, representing more than 85% of U.S. Catholics, adopted and implemented the *PGCA* program and as of 2022, over 5 million adult Catholics have been through the program. However, because dioceses were *mandating* the program, a key step—the "buy in"—was missing from the original implementation plan. There was no campaign to enroll the people in local parishes in the value and importance of participating and the response was often less than enthusiastic.

PGCA was designed to educate interested adults about a serious public health problem and teach them how to prevent this kind of child abuse. Instead, resentment and resistance were frequent responses from the people. They only came to the sessions because they were told it was required. If they refused or failed to participate, they could not participate in staff or volunteer positions in ministries and activities for children and youth. It is also true that although most people arrived at the awareness session in a less than enthusiastic mood, once they saw the program, their attitude changed significantly. They saw value in the awareness session and were glad they had the opportunity to come.

However, many still were not eager to do the training necessary to become proficient with the tools provided in the session.

Regardless of how much they agreed the program was valuable and worth the time they spent at the presentation, they still were not convinced of the need for further training. In their opinion, they now had enough information to protect children.

The objective of raising *awareness* was being achieved at a rate that was almost unimaginable to the design and development teams, but a one-time program does not change *behavior*—and a behavior change was needed to accomplish the ultimate goal of preventing child sexual abuse. That becomes possible only when people are able to assimilate the tools in the program into their day-to-day interactions with others. Training was required to bring that about. Training and practice are what allows adults to recognize potentially risky behavior and intervene before abuse occurs.

After observing the responses of adult participants to the program, it became clear that the message that all children are at risk and it is the job of adults to protect them was being heard. Parents were asking more questions and sending emails and comments to the program experts looking for answers to the questions about how to make sure their children are safe from child sexual abuse. However, the simple answer—take advantage of the training and become expert at screening adults in your environment—was not being heard by most of the faith community. Clergy, staff, program facilitators, educators, youth ministers, and others with direct responsibility for children in the parish or school were participating in the training but parents and other adult volunteers were not.

Most seemed to think that the information they got in the awareness session was all they needed. Now that they knew the risks, they would be more attentive and careful about the other adults in their child's environment—and they probably are. However, simply paying attention to the things they remembered from the awareness session is not enough to change behavior or allow all adults to develop a real ability to identify potential child molesters and stop the abuse before it happened.

The question

In the midst of examining this dilemma, a question began to emerge for me about how we adults develop know-how in certain areas of our life. How do we acquire the ability to see the potential risks of harm in a situation or circumstance and prevent damage or disaster from occurring?

Looking at those areas of life where we seem to have the ability to see what's coming and avoid harm, new questions began to arise:

- Do human beings have a set of undefined skills that we rely on to develop those areas of life?
- If so, can we identify these skills in a way that makes them available to us to apply in other areas of life?

Examining my own areas of expertise I began to recognize certain skills that were applied to the learning process in these areas of life. Investigating this possibility could determine whether these skills or processes were unique to one person or common to each of us. The answer to that question could provide a valuable resource for all adults and children.

A set of survey questions was developed and sent to a number of people in different professions with varying areas of interest who agreed to be interviewed for the project. The inquiry was unique because the questions were designed to provoke a unique look at how individuals accomplish objectives and build proficiencies. The questions gave each person an opportunity to look carefully at how they acquire expertise—not what they know or how they use their expertise.

In the next chapter we examine the process of gathering the information on which the theory of *20/20 Foresight* is based and the questions each interviewee was asked to consider.

CHAPTER THREE

The Research

On the one hand, the guidelines for conducting traditional research that I learned in graduate school were helpful in my efforts to conduct the study into how people develop expertise in an area they are interested in. However, the question was unique and required a customized approach. It was not simply about gathering data and information. I needed people to think through something they had not been asked to consider before.

What I created was a three-step process. In Step 1, I created a list of people who might be willing to participate. The only criterion for selection was that each one has a different area of interest or expertise. The areas of expertise were related to job or vocation as well as hobbies, games, and other interests.

Locating people was easy. Everyone I asked was intrigued by the question I was asking and readily volunteered to be part of the research.

Once I lined up the people, Step 2 was providing them with some written background information about what I was up to and what I wanted to look at. Then each one got a list of questions designed to stimulate thinking about this subject in a new and different way. The questions were sent out approximately five days before Step 3 so that each person had the same amount of time to consider their answers and the questions were still fresh at the time we talked.

Step 3 was a personal interview during which the people being interviewed had a chance to really explore how they learn and develop expertise, skill, and competence in certain areas of life.

Responding to the questions generally was quite challenging for everyone. We all discovered that although people often deal with

17

questions about "how" they do what they do, no one was asking them how they got to be experts at what they do.

Mechanics are accustomed to questions about how to fix something in the car and computer software designers are often asked how to revise a program to make it do something different. These questions were different and were designed to explore something unique – a question they had never been asked before.

In order to ensure that the research had integrity, and everyone had an opportunity to really see for themselves whether there was a process to developing this kind of expertise, some safeguards were built into the interview process. First, I conducted all the interviews myself. So, in every case, the interviewer was the same person, and the questions were asked the same way.

Second, most of the interviews were taped so there was a record of the conversation that could substantiate what was said by both participants.

Third, the questions asked were the ones the participants had already had a chance to look at before the interview. Even then, the answers started to drift into areas of "how" the person did the job or played the game. It was important to steer people back to a discussion of how they developed the skill and ability to do what they do rather than the mechanics of how they do what they do.

The Guinea Pigs

As I said earlier, it was easy to find people who wanted to be part of the project. Perhaps one of the reasons was that the standard for selecting people was simple. First, the person had to be willing to participate. Second, they needed to have expertise in some area of life. Third, their area of expertise needed to be different from anyone else's who was volunteering for the project.

There were no educational requirements. There were no other conditions the participants had to meet or agree to. In fact, there was a deliberate attempt to make sure there were a variety of interests, backgrounds, and activities represented by the interview subjects.

Diversity of interests was important because the question was not about delving into the way something gets done; it was about seeing whether there was a method or pattern in the way we become proficient.

Some interviewees were chosen because they are experts in a hobby or leisure activity, while others were chosen because of their level of proficiency in their job, vocation, or avocation. In addition, no participant was given the names of any others who were part of the project before they were interviewed. In this way, there was no discussion between the participants about the process, the interview, and what they saw until after their interview was completed.

Everyone invited to participate was enthusiastic about the project and intrigued by the questions. At some time during each interview, participants commented about the uniqueness of the questions and the fact that they had never looked at things in that way before.

The interviews were challenging and creative. Because this was a new view of things for everyone involved, none of the answers came easy. One of my challenges was to keep quiet and let people struggle with the questions, so the process took something on both my part and that of the person being interviewed. It also was challenging to keep the discussion focused on the issues at hand, leading the way for the people being interviewed to see something that they had not seen before and to find answers to question that previously had never come up.

The brave souls who lent themselves to this process included:

- Kathy—A pharmacist whose commitment to her patients is well known among both the people in the community and her colleagues in the medical community. In addition to running two pharmacies and being a parent, she has completed a Doctorate in Pharmacy and recently published her first book.
- Patrick—An entrepreneur who has imagined, developed, operated, and sold several businesses over time. His ability in business and his expert judgment allows him to focus his energy on developing something new and/or taking something that was failing and turning it into something great.
- Diane—A software designer for a major player in the oil, gas, and water processing industry. Diane ventured into the world of computers years ago when computers were just coming into the forefront of society and business. She was curious and had an adventuresome nature and it led her to a new job and a new career. This adventuresome spirit frequently moves her to try new things and pursue interesting questions.
- Mary—A lawyer whose particular areas of concentration include mediation and adoption. She is one of 11 children and used the inquiry to look at several areas of proficiency in her life including the role she plays in her family, being a mother, her participation in church activities, as well as the areas of emphasis in her legal career.
- Charles—Although he was at the time of the initial interview a building and materials administrator/manager for a public school system, this interviewee is also a master carpenter who previously owned and operated a construction company and built custom furniture. He looked at all of these areas to see commonalities in the way he develops proficiencies.
- Marty—A family practice physician who began his career in the medical profession as a pharmaceutical representative and who also served as a Cobra attack helicopter pilot during the Viet Nam war. He used the questions to look at both his development as a physician and how he assesses and applies new information that comes his way through medical journals, pharmaceutical representatives, etc.

- Chris—A commercial pilot for a major airline who also spent several years as a pilot for the U.S. Air Force. In addition to flying fighter planes for the Air Force, he was an Instructor Pilot and trained many others before leaving the military to become part of the commercial airline industry. His safety record as a pilot is impeccable.
- Brian—A computer game expert who started playing computer games as a teenager. A serious health condition he inherited from his father prevented him from participating in other sports activities. He started playing games with his friends at home on the TV in the den and now plays with friends around the world on the Internet.
- Shannon—An IT executive who also has a Masters in Developmental Psychology, is an accomplished researcher, writes fiction, and is an expert at cross-stitch.
- Nancy—A master trainer who has worked with local, national, and international companies. Her expertise in this field has led her to develop a unique system that allows her to prepare and conduct highly effective training sessions using materials provided from another source.
- Dave—An entrepreneur who, as a fish wholesaler, was responsible for creating the process by which Americans could get fresh Chilean sea bass, swordfish, and other treats in fine dining restaurants and fish markets across the country. He then moved on to a new venture and, began buying and renovating hotels.
- John—A management consultant who specializes in empowering smaller companies to reorganize, expand, and build on their past successes. He is also a guitarist who is brushing up on this skill and reestablishing his expertise so he can play for his grandchildren.
- JoAnn—an artist who is an accomplished water colorist and who is in the midst of changing to a new medium. She was able to look at the questions from two different perspectives as she is dealing with one area of established skill and another area where she is developing that expression of her artistic abilities.
- Tomme—A gifted lawyer who was employed as a law clerk for a Federal Magistrate Judge in the central United States and is now retired to the Pacific Northwest. She is also an accomplished pianist, a Yoga instructor, and a

talented quilter sewing magnificent works of art with fabric. She focused her inquiry on how she acquired skills and abilities as a quilter.

- Jeff—A talented journalist, business consultant, and webmaster who developed programs for businesses and created and edited content for websites. He also was trained to provide services as a bodyguard for a state official, and he applied the questions and the inquiry to the training received for that responsibility.
- Cathy—A lawyer who is also a master trainer with a great deal of experience in ministry with teens. She has a proven track record of developing a remarkable level of proficiency in any area of interest that she takes on.

Each person received the following document, which contained the background information and the questions. As mentioned earlier, the information and the specific questions were designed to provoke the participants' thinking about their own expertise from an entirely different perspective.

BACKGROUND:

We all are familiar with the accuracy of 20/20 hindsight. Looking back, we can see every wrong step we took and everything we missed. We know what they and we should have done or said and we can see where it all went off the mark.

However, consider that, in some specific areas of your life, you also have what I call 20/20 *Foresight. In those areas of life, such as in your work/profession, you look for and often can see potentially risky situations or circumstances before they happen, and you intervene to make sure everything works out.*

The theory I am working on is that this ability is derived from a skill set human beings have—but do not relate to as a skill set. We think we are just good at our job, or we have done something so often or worked at learning it so well that it has become second nature to us. Perhaps this is not the case. Perhaps, if we can identify and hone this set of skills, we have the ability to bring them to bear on areas of our life where we don't seem to have the same facility with seeing the possible problems and resolving them in advance.

There is at least one precedent for our ability to develop this type of Foresight—defensive driving. Day after day, millions of cars fill our freeways, highways, and neighborhood streets. Every day, most of those millions of cars safely traverse traffic-filled roads and arrive at their destinations with fenders and passengers intact. However, there also are often moments during those trips when the driver heaves a sigh of relief and thanks God that he or she survived a "near miss." Consider that those "near misses" are an example of what I am calling "20/20 Foresight" in action. In those moments, the driver recognized the advance warning signs of a potentially risky situation and took action to avoid an accident. By knowing the warning signs of potential danger on the highway, and acting automatically in response to those signs, drivers avoid many would-be accidents.

I am interviewing a number of people in different professions in an effort to identify the specific aspects of the skill set that we draw on in those specific areas. I appreciate your willingness to participate in this project.

The following questions were drafted to help you think about the learning process you use to develop your expertise. Remember that I am interested in how you developed the proficiency, rather than the specific knowledge, that you have in your area of expertise. Thank you in advance for playing a part in the investigation of my 20/20 Foresight theory.

SURVEY QUESTIONS:

1. What are the steps you take when you are learning something in which you plan to develop proficiency?

2. In an area of life where you operate with proficiency:
    a. How did you learn the basics?
    b. How did you decide what was important to remember?
    c. What did you have your eye/attention on when you were starting out?
    d. Where did you focus your attention once you learned the basic skills?

3. How did you develop and expand your ability to think through potential problems?

4. How do you identify the warning signs that something is headed in the wrong direction?

5. How do you look for these signs when you are engaged in this activity?

23

6.   *How long did it take before you began to see potential risks and intervene automatically?*

7.   *What else do you have to say about the learning process that has allowed you to develop proficiency in your chosen field?*

8.   *If you look at other areas in which you have become proficient, whether they relate to your career, or even a hobby or other interest, do you see the basic steps on the road toward proficiency as being similar or different, and why?*

A lot of people have given at least some thought to how they do what they do. There has also been a great deal of research on how we learn. The ways that adults learn seem to be particularly important to the people who develop programs for adult learning—as well as those who write ads for commercials. Everything from advertising for cereal to do-it-yourself seminars at nationally known home improvement stores is designed to make the greatest impact on the listener, viewer, or reader—depending on which one you are.

So what is it that experts know about how we adults learn anyway? Howard Gardner, PhD, a developmental psychologist from Harvard University says that each person has several different ways that we learn.[vii] These commonly are referred to as:[viii]

- Visual—Primary learning style is through pictures and images.
- Aural—Learns best by listening. Sound and music is the key.
- Verbal—Speaking and writing are the most effective tools for learning.
- Physical—Physical contact and a sense of touch are the most effective ways to learn.
- Logical—Logic and reasoning provide the best access to learning.
- Social—Group work with other people makes the most of a learning situation.
- Solitary—Working alone and engaging in self-study is the preferred method.

Each of us can learn using any of these methods as described by Dr. Gardner. However, for each of us, there is one particular style that works best. In other words, there is a way information is presented to us that allows us to get the most out of what is offered.

The thing to remember is that these learning styles tell us about the most effective way for each of us to absorb information and retain it for future use. They don't tell us much about how we become experts or gain working knowledge that allows us to identify potential risks on the horizon and avoid any approaching danger. Incorporating what we learn into our thinking patterns in such a way that we are able to identify potential risks and intervene to prevent damage clearly requires more than gathering information.

Interestingly, Dr. Gardner's work in this area was motivated by a desire to give his children the door to developing aptitude and know-how in areas of their lives. He wanted to give them tools to help them avoid mistakes, deal with risky situations, and move forward in their endeavors. In his words:

> *I want my children to understand the world, but not just because the world is fascinating, and the human mind is curious. I want them to understand it so that they will be positioned to make it a better place. Knowledge is not the same as morality, but we need to understand if we are to avoid past mistakes and move in productive directions. An important part of that understanding is knowing who we are and what we can do... Ultimately, we must synthesize our understandings for ourselves. The performance of understanding that try matters are the ones we carry out as human beings in an imperfect world, which we can affect for good or for ill. (Howard Gardner 1999: 180-181)*

We all know that acquiring knowledge or information is valuable, but something more is needed if we are to develop proficiencies. Knowing about the different ways we absorb information is an important part of the learning process. However, when considering how they built proficiencies, the project participants first looked at how they do what they do—the process they use to "get the job done." For most, the first answer was, "It is just the way that I do it." It did not seem unusual. In fact, it seemed as if they were simply doing what came naturally.

Although they understood how they learned, they had never looked at just how they got to that place. They never even thought about how they take information or knowledge and develop it into the ability, for example, to recognize potentially risky or dangerous situations and take appropriate action to avoid the risk or danger. In fact, one of the first things the participants saw was that they operate on "automatic" when they notice something is off or they see a potential problem on the horizon. They saw that they react to situations rather than making a conscious decision to act.

Looking at and thinking about these new questions allowed for a new perspective, a whole new view of the way they operate in life. During the process, most admitted they had never considered how they developed the ability to see those red flags on the horizon and take action to prevent a problem or even stop a disaster from happening. They simply never looked at themselves and how they function on a day-to-day basis from this perspective.

Although it was challenging, one key aspect of the interview process was keeping the participants on point. It is instinctive for us to talk about what we know. Everyone wants to appear knowledgeable and articulate in an interview. These participants were no different—and talking about what they know how to do and how they accomplish objectives was very comfortable for each of them.

It was up to me to keep encouraging the participants to talk without suggesting any answers to the questions. Some of the interviews were conducted in person and others by telephone, and all were completed in late 2005 and early 2006. The process and what was discovered were enlightening and exciting.

CHAPTER FOUR

The Tools Identified

During the interviews, each person went through a unique process of analysis. However, the results were so similar that it was exciting and enlightening. Every person identified specific steps they took to develop proficiencies in designated areas of their life. The steps were the same for every participant even though they often used different words to describe them.

For example, one might say, "I ask for what I need," and another might say, "I gather all the relevant information." However, when they clarified the process further, it became clear that each one was describing how they gather information from various resources that would be helpful in developing proficiency. They might each be relying on the most effective and efficient way they learn but the step was all about gathering information.

Another similarity was that although not everyone talked about the steps in the same order or in an orderly manner, they eventually doubled back to fill in the gaps. For example, they might start by talking about practice and repetition as a key but eventually they realized that first there was a reason to practice, and second there was learning enough about the subject to make practicing worthwhile.

It became clear after only a few interviews that a pattern was emerging—a pattern that was clear and unequivocal. Based on the experiences of the people interviewed, there is a process—a series of steps and tools that we human beings employ to develop expertise in areas of our life. The tools we identified demonstrate that there is a design to the process of developing competence of the highest levels. Simply stated, the skills, tools, or steps that we apply when we are building our expertise in an area are:

1. A compelling interest or passion
2. Gathering information
3. Practice
4. Paying attention
5. Being flexible
6. Operating in the "zone"

By the end of each interview, each participant had spoken about all six of these elements as integral parts of the process. They recognized that every one of these steps was key to developing their expertise or building a proficiency. They could also see that, in reality, they followed the steps in order to get to the ultimate goal.

For example, they all saw that the real reason they had a commitment to practice in this particular area of life is that they had a compelling interest or passion about something. They were able to see that without this compelling interest or passion, their interest in a subject waned over time and eventually disappeared. Perhaps this begins to explain why action taken to fulfill a New Year's resolution that is made with the best of intentions begins with enthusiasm but fades into the background at the first bump in the road.

In later chapters we will discuss each of the steps in detail and look at the various ways they are applied by different people to achieve the same result. We also will take a look at how we can use this knowledge and information to be more effective at developing proficiencies in our lives, particularly in areas where we have faltered in the past.

CHAPTER FIVE

A Compelling Interest

Why does one person become passionate about antiques while another focuses on creating cutting-edge technology? Why does one person's New Year's resolution to go to the gym turn into a commitment to building a healthy body while another with the same resolution gets sidetracked and gives up after three weeks? Although the answer to these questions is somewhat illusive, it is clear from the interviews conducted that in those instances when the interest becomes a passion and the good idea becomes an unwavering commitment, at some point, the person has acquired a compelling interest or passion about the subject. It may be that someone is just drawn to a particular subject or that they see something challenging or beautiful or interesting that bears investigation. It may be simply that people can see that developing know-how and expertise in a particular area is in their best interest or would make a difference for their families or in their job. In that case, they use this realization as their motivating factor and make a determined effort to become skilled in this area.

However, in the process of identifying and clarifying the skills they used to develop expertise in a particular area, the answer to the question "why" do I have a compelling interest about this subject is less relevant than "how" do I develop a compelling interest. What's important is to know that in every single case, the compelling interest or passion was necessary if the person was to acquire any real ability or develop any meaningful proficiency.

The participants agreed that the starting point for developing a skill that rises to the level of *20/20 Foresight* is having a compelling interest in or a passion for that particular "thing." The participants also were clear that having this compelling interest or passion was not necessarily something that just happened. This compelling interest or passion could come from a variety of sources and be driven by a number of factors. Some are obvious and others seem illusive but there is something that compels us to move forward through the steps to proficiency.

The compelling interest might arise because the person has become fascinated with something such as a hobby or career choice. Most mechanics are fascinated by the way a vehicle works. Many of them have spent their whole lives taking things apart and putting them back together. From the time they were very young, my son and his best friend were always taking something apart on the driveway and putting it back together. Bicycles, motorcycles, cars, and trucks in their possession all ended up dismantled and then reassembled at some point. Today, my son is a network administrator for a midsized corporation—building computer networks and systems that operate many aspects of the business—and in his spare time, he rebuilds cars. His best friend owns a car repair shop and makes his living doing what he has loved to do since he was a young boy.

Maybe their interest in cars was born out of their fascination with the way things work. Maybe it was just that they got interested in working on cars because they were best friends and what one cared about was also important to the other. There is no rhyme or reason to the way this passion or interest develops but developing this type of interest is essential to the process.

Our airline pilot, Chris, can't remember a time when he was not passionate about flying, airplanes, and air travel. This "passion" for flying has colored every educational and career decision he has made in his life. His passion for flying is infectious. It is not limited to being in the pilot's seat. He also has a brokerage business and guess what he brokers—airplanes. One of his goals was create opportunities for physically and emotionally challenged and at-risk young people and teens to discover flying so he and his wife and children volunteer their time and resources to an organization called Challenge Air that makes that experience available and use their own plane to make "Angel flights" for those with special medical needs.

The catalyst for Brian, the video game expert, was entirely different. He developed an interest in "gaming" because he was afflicted with a genetic disorder that prevented him from participating in regular team sports. He has Marfan's Syndrome, which is a disorder of the connective tissue—the material that holds us together. Although people with the disorder can function fairly normally, excess exertion such as competitive sports can cause substantial damage to the body—and substantial damage to his body can result in death. Because he could not actively engage in the same sports that others were playing and because he loved to read and had an active imagination, video games became his passion. They were new, they were cool, and they were a way that he and his buddies could do something together that was challenging, competitive, and fun.

Others were more practical in their approach. They relied more on identifying a self-interest in pursuing a particular interest area than on their "feelings" about something. Charles saw that throughout his life, he had taken on the task of acquiring know-how when a need or a crisis arose and it was up to him to respond. In his world, it was just what there was to do, and because he was not raised to do anything halfway, he created a self-interest that would motivate him to develop proficiency in that area. As a result, he is someone who feels comfortable with dynamic situations and depends on himself to establish the solid ground on which he stands on a daily basis.

Mary observed that from early on in life, she noticed that she preferred to listen and observe to find out what others needed and then provide it. She also saw that it was in her self-interest to do so. As one of eleven children, this course of action often had her in the background, quietly producing really good grades and causing very little trouble for her parents and siblings. As she pursued this course of action and realized that she was good at it, this became her standard for choosing an interest to pursue. It is not surprising that she eventually became an attorney with an emphasis on mediation and adoption. You can be sure that Mary deliberately avoids the adversarial litigation process.

In some cases, the interest or passion grew out of a determination that the subject matter or issue included information that either would provide personal gain or would make a difference for others in the person's life. For example, when our physician, Marty, pondered the interview questions, he saw that he has a set of criteria for determining whether to learn about a new drug or to develop a proficiency in a new procedure. First, he looks to see whether the new drug or procedure would make a difference for his patients. New medication and new procedures for treating rheumatoid arthritis are valuable—but not necessarily for a family practice physician who refers those patients to a specialist for treatment. However, new blood pressure medication or a new treatment for gout is a different matter altogether.

The process doesn't stop there though. If the product passes the first test and Marty sees that the new drug or procedure could make a difference for his patients, he moves on to the next part of the analysis. He examines his own existing level of competence about the health issue at hand and then looks at his past experience with the source of the information, the drug, or the procedure. Has this company provided him with good information and valuable methods in the past? Is this new procedure a product of good research and development?

Finally, he looks to see the broader impact of the new drug or new procedure on society. "Will there be an enhancement of the quality of life for the people in my practice if I focus my attention on learning all I need to know about this drug or developing proficiency with this new procedure?" If the answer to all these questions is "yes," then our doctor moves on in the process of becoming proficient with this drug or this new technique. It is through this process that he develops a compelling interest that is the first step to becoming proficient with the drug or procedure.

Although the process used by the physician is methodical, thoughtful, and multifaceted, it is, in many ways, no different than the process used by the trained bodyguard who evaluated where to place his time and energy based on one basic criterion—the safety and well-being of his client. Jeff was educated as a journalist and never aspired to be a bodyguard. However, when he found himself in a situation where his life and the life of the person he worked for were being threatened, he developed a compelling interest in being a very good bodyguard.

Jeff told me that for a bodyguard, the only concern is the well-being of the person he or she is protecting. Ironically, the bodyguard asks questions that are similar, in many ways, to Marty's questions about whether the new drug or procedure will make a difference for his patients. Each of them looked first to determine whether there was a reason to turn their attention to becoming knowledgeable or proficient about the thing. They each had their own criteria for answering that question, but once the answer was "yes," there was a compelling interest in developing a competency and eventually being able to rely on a certain level of expertise.

One person admitted that a major factor for her in determining whether to nurture and develop an interest in an area was a desire to please others. Similar to the lawyer, doctor, and bodyguard, this participant looked to the needs of those around her to determine which areas or issues deserved this kind of focused attention.

Some people experienced what they could only describe as a "burning desire," something that pulled them forward into action. Still others discovered that they seemed to have a talent or a gift for something and that was the motivating force behind their burgeoning interest.

JoAnn could not imagine her life without paintbrushes and blank canvases. At the time of our interview, she was already an accomplished water color artist. However, she found herself taking up an entirely new medium. She was in the midst of learning this new medium and since our initial interview her oil paintings are already selling.

She described both the need to create art and the need to learn a new medium as "burning desires." In her experience, there was just no way to ignore or avoid the pull to paint and create art. When asked why, after years of working in one medium, she suddenly was drawn to a new medium of expression for her art, the answer was simple: she saw and admired the work of another artist. That was enough to spark her interest.

Although it may seem odd, Diane, the software programmer, saw something similar when she looked to see where it all began for her. She saw that, in the early days of computer programming, the idea of it was fun and exciting to her. She had a career and she was good at it. What intrigued her about changing careers was that she saw this new area as stimulating and she could see that becoming skilled in this area would allow her to create something and then see it work. That stirred her adventurous side.

Shannon found her "muse" in developing what she considered to be "survival skills," the skills she needs to survive in her own environment. In her case, those skills include such things as developing a proficiency in her job so that she survives and thrives in the work environment and, at the same time, learning how to thrive and flourish while also dealing with a husband with a chronic health issue.

Still another participant, John, saw that his main concern was using his time for things that are important to him. However, during the conversation, it became clear that this did not necessarily mean he was selfish. It turns out this middle-aged management consultant was relearning how to play the guitar and sing. In his younger days, he played guitar in a rock band but he had put that part of his life aside some time ago. Now he had a young grandson and he discovered that he wanted to play for this new member of the family so he began practicing and renewing his skills with the guitar. It seems that after his grandson was born he remembered the joy of the time he spent playing and singing to his newborn son. In that moment, playing the guitar suddenly became important to him again.

Every person interviewed agreed that developing expertise in any area of life begins with building on a foundation that is rooted in a special interest or passion about something. There must be, at some level, an intense desire to do the work necessary to develop proficiency. It is this compelling interest or passion that lays the foundation for the work that is necessary to finally achieve a level of proficiency that allows us to trust our instincts and react well to problems.

This foundation is the framework for the process going forward. Without the foundation, there is nothing to hold the process together. Without the foundation, there is no framework for success. This explains why a New Year's resolution based on "should" or "ought to" has no staying power.

The thing to remember is that there is no "right way" to develop a compelling interest or passion for something. Perhaps it is as simple as identifying whether and how a particular area will support you in fulfilling your dreams and goals. Several years ago, a young executive in a very high-energy job shared with me that she had some health problems that were positively impacted if she ate three times a day. Her bosses and co-workers knew this and they asked her to promise to take care of herself as part of her work responsibilities. Almost every day, someone would ask whether she was eating regularly and, every day the answer was the same—"no." Finally, she said, her manager told her either to find a way to do what she said she would do or stop pretending that she was going to do it because it was clear that this way of dealing with it was not producing any results and everyone was simply becoming more frustrated.

She realized that she had no compelling interest in food. In fact, she did not care about eating at all. Therefore, she was only promising to eat in order to make them happy—and that did not motivate her to action. However, she also knew that eating regularly was in her best interest, so she began to look for a reason that would motivate her to eat properly, and she found it. She saw that the only way to accomplish her purpose in life was with a body that supported her in that effort. She also saw that without a healthy and physically functioning body, she would not be able to make the kind of difference she was committed to making. In the moment she came to that realization, her attitude about eating shifted. She now had a compelling interest and no one ever had to remind her to eat properly again.

Without this compelling interest, passion, or burning desire, there is nothing pulling us to take the actions necessary to develop a proficiency. Whether this interest is created from something intuitive or because we see the value for our own lives or the lives of those around us is not important. What is important is establishing that interest or identifying that passion or desire. That is the foundation—the first step in developing a high level of expertise in any area of life.

CHAPTER SIX

Gathering Information

Think back to a time when you first saw or heard something that piqued an interest and you could not wait to learn more. The experience was similar to hunger—a hunger for information. You looked everywhere for more and more and more information including basic data as well as practical knowledge and experience. You were like a child experiencing something for the first time, and you searched out every possible avenue of information and resource in your quest for information. You were fascinated and the more you learned, the more you wanted to know.

During that time, you found all sorts of ways to gather information. You talked with other people who had knowledge, experience, or expertise. You kept an eye out for anything that could teach you more or help you gain expertise. You took classes, read books and articles on the subject, and talked with people with similar interests to learn all that you could about this new area of interest. All of this was part of gathering information, the second step in the process of developing *20/20 Foresight*—and to you it just seemed like the logical and natural way to pursue this interest.

There are many, many ways we gather information. Not all of them are obvious nor do all of them lead us to become experts about something. We gather information from a variety of sources for many different reasons. Every day, we are inundated with more and more information. Some have called this the "Information Age" because of the amount of data that is coming at us each day.

Although most of us don't think of ourselves in this way, we human beings know a lot about a lot of things. The problem is we also demonstrate, over and over again, day after day, that knowing something usually makes no real difference.

For example, most of us who are overweight know how to lose weight; most people are clear about the value of healthy exercise and, in today's world no one really thinks smoking is good for us. We know that tobacco related illnesses are among the leading causes of death for adults.[ix] In spite of all this knowledge we can't seem to stop overeating, we seem to have no trouble at all abandoning that new exercise plan and, according to the Centers for Disease Control an estimated 34.1 adults in the United States still smoked as of 2018.[x] That accounts for 15.6% of all men and 12% of all adult women. Even though those numbers have declined approximately 5% since 2005, there were still 480,000 deaths from smoking related causes in 2018. That means that 1 in 5 deaths were attributed to smoking.[xi]

So, if gathering information were just about accumulating knowledge, the odds are that ultimately it would make no difference.[xii] During my interview with John, our management consultant, he talked about this very issue. He said that in his experience, the difference between acquiring knowledge and really learning something is that although he can get his hands on knowledge about almost anything, having the information doesn't mean he can do something or use the information in real life situations. When he has really learned something, the information gained is useful and he relies on it to make decisions and to take actions in certain circumstances.

If you recall, John took up the guitar again in order to be able to play it for his new grandson. This difference between knowledge and learning that John spoke about is the difference between knowing the fingering for chords on the guitar and having your hands automatically go to that location on the fingerboard when you see the music.

John once again is going from knowing how to play the guitar to playing the guitar and enjoying this activity with his grandson and family. Knowing where to put his fingers on the fingerboard doesn't create music. Developing the know-how and ability to do that automatically does not come automatically once you know something.

When the need to get information is driven by a compelling interest or passion something completely different happens. In those instances, the need to have more information is a critical piece of the process, but it is not the end of the process. In fact, it is just the beginning. It is also no longer just a good idea or something we might do;

it is a necessary building block in our effort to develop the kind of ability and skill that qualifies as expertise.

When a compelling interest or passion is driving us, the interest in gathering information and developing resources never wanes. In fact, we often develop a new level of efficiency and skill in gathering information and assimilating it into our thought processes.

The interesting thing about this piece of the puzzle in developing *20/20 Foresight* is that, although our interest in new information and resources never fades, it also does not occur to us as education or training or something we are required to do. It is not a burden to do this.

We don't even think about this step in the process in terms of "taking classes" or "going to school" because we should or because we need to. We certainly don't find anything odd about reading a trade magazine for fun or spending Saturday morning watching a presentation on public television or the Discovery Channel about new quilting techniques or ideas for an innovative model train layout.

Pilots may decorate their homes with art that has an airplane theme and read everything that comes out about new ideas in aviation. Those with a passion for Africa or the Orient or antiques have homes that are filled with that décor—and the homeowner can tell you everything you want to know about the items that are on display.

In spite of the fact that these participants were extremely knowledgeable and very skilled in certain areas of their lives, some of them found it very hard to admit they had acquired *any* real competence or they could be considered an expert in anything. When we talked about why this was the case, they each reached the same conclusion. They were afraid that labeling themselves as proficient would impact their interest in and ability to continue to gather information. They thought thinking of themselves as "experts" somehow would give them permission to slack off and coast on what they already know. It was as if they saw recognizing and acknowledging a certain level of competency as the death knell for continued growth and development. Because none of them wanted to stop growing and learning and becoming more skilled in the areas they are passionate about, they didn't want to risk any chance that they might back off or begin to think they have something handled.

The process of acquiring and maintaining this type of proficiency places a premium on continuing to acquire knowledge and information. New information that becomes part of the background of our thinking expands our ability to recognize potentially risky situations and avert disaster—and allows us to continue to build on the foundation of knowledge and information that we have already gathered. Even someone others think of as a "know it all" can't stop the quest for additional information, new insights, new ideas, and increasing their knowledge base when they have a compelling interest in something or they are passionate about it.

Furthermore, this quest has virtually no boundaries. Participants make use of a wide variety of "gathering" tools to enhance their knowledge and understanding of their area of interest and continue to build proficiency. Some tools are more formalized or traditional learning methods. Others are more spontaneous and thought provoking. The two things these "gathering tools" have in common are that they appeal to the person with the compelling interest, and they expand on existing information for the person using them.

The formal "gathering" tools

The variety of tools we use to gather information on the road to becoming an expert is unmatched in any other project, goal, or objective that we undertake. The participants who were interviewed for this book were creative in their search for information. They demonstrated many, many ways of gathering knowledge as they went through the process. They were also clear in their commitment to leave no stone unturned in the learning process.

a. Taking Classes

It almost goes without saying that everyone started by laying a solid foundation of basic information. A starting place for many was participation in formal education classes of one type or another. Classes as part of a higher education program, classes in technology or technical training schools, and classes as part of adult public and private continuing education programs were frequently part of the process of gathering basic information.

Kathy, who is already a licensed pharmacist and the owner of two thriving pharmacies, returned to school in later years to complete a Doctorate in Pharmacy. It was not something she needed to succeed. However, it was something she felt drawn to do because of her passion for her patients and her commitment to provide them with the very best care.

Another participant has four different degrees in four different areas of educational endeavor. She has obviously chosen formal education processes as the starting place for developing whatever expertise and proficiency she has gained in the last 40 years—and she still has trouble considering herself an expert in any of these disciplines.

An additional aspect of formal education that was evident in the information gathering process was attendance at continuing education seminars and workshops. We seek out continuing education opportunities in the areas we are passionate about. We often will go out of our way or sacrifice other things to have the opportunity to listen to someone we admire as an expert in the field or to hear about a new theory or new procedure that can enhance our capabilities in this area. We take seminars to learn "more" about the subject matter, more about how it works, more about how to "do" it, more about what it includes, more about what is known about it, or more about how it developed.

The willingness or need to learn something new or gather more formal education never stops. Programs like "Road Scholar" offer travel to fascinating new places coupled with insightful educational programs—all available only to the over 55 crowd.[xiii] We seek out new or additional information regardless of whether our interests are found in more formal areas of education such as computer programming, engineering, or management, or in the more informal areas of interest such as quilting or building playground equipment for the back yard.

One of the types of formal learning that has developed and become very popular in recent years is through the Internet. Seminars conducted online in real time make courses and workshops available to a wide audience that was never contemplated in the past. Public television was a great resource for many years but now that too has expanded. Now we can add the Discovery Channel, TLC, Bravo, the Food Network, Animal Planet channel, Court TV, ESPN, USA, HGTV, and many others to opportunities for gathering information from a more formal source.

b. Looking for Experts

Although we rarely consider ourselves to be experts, as part of the formal process of learning, we do look for others whom we consider to be "experts" to talk to, listen to, and observe. Identifying experts begins with establishing criteria for knowing how to identify an "expert" in our particular area of interest. The criteria could vary depending on the area we are studying. A high level of quality craftsmanship in a finished product may lead us to an expert cabinetmaker, seamstress, or jewelry designer. Academic credentials, publications, and professional reputation may be the standards for experts in such areas as forensic anthropology, music history, or child abuse prevention. Some expert criteria will require both intellectual and tangible standards.

These experts we are seeking may have concentrated knowledge in the specific area of our interest, or they may have talents in areas or subjects that are related to our particular area of interest. For example, if you are interested in model trains, someone who is an expert at building landscape models out of Paper Mache is an expert in a related area. Knowing how to build these landscapes is an important part of creating an interesting and fun layout for a model train.

Identifying experts is one way to research the area. It is, for many, the initial attempt at what one participant called "building the pyramid" of knowledge. Identifying experts is part of building a solid foundation. But it is only one element of a much broader and diverse effort to collect information.

Expert writings, research, and conversation can provide information that dispels confusion and encourages continued exploration into the subject matter. The purpose of identifying and tapping into expertise is two-fold. The first and most obvious purpose of this tool is to "gather" information. Experts provide a wealth of knowledge about a subject and this knowledge is invaluable to us, particularly during this initial part of the process.

A second and equally valuable use of experts is to begin to draw on their knowledge and experience to identify potential problems or apparently risky situations. If we want to be truly skillful in any area of life or have expertise on any subject, we need to be able to recognize and avoid potential problems and identify and deal with possible risks of harm or damage before they happen. Experts can help us begin to clarify potential pitfalls and problems and take appropriate action to avert disaster or damage of any kind.

Formal avenues for gathering information are valuable assets to anyone who wants to learn something new or who become interested in a new area or develops a new passion. However, formal processes of gathering information such as attending classes or seminars or consulting experts are just some of the tools we use to gather information.

Informal Gathering Tools

Real expertise takes something more than classroom study and learning from the experts. One research participant described the process of reaching out for information in all directions as similar to the octopus with tentacles reaching out in many directions at the same time. The octopus knows what it is looking for—food and more of it—but it has no specific idea where to find what it needs, so it spreads out in many different directions on the chance that something of value will show up.

An inquisitive mind and a willingness to look for answers and information anywhere you can find it leads you down the pathway to developing *20/20 Foresight*. One of the ways to make sure you are getting the most out of your efforts is to bring what the great Zen masters call a "beginner's mind" to each step in the learning process.[xiv]

A beginner's mind is one that is interested and open. It "is empty, free of the habits of the expert, ready to accept, to doubt, and open to all possibilities."[xv] It is the kind of mind that can see things as they are and take it all in without judgment or assessment.[xvi]

Bringing a beginner's mind to each level of the process of developing *20/20 Foresight* does not mean forgetting what you already know. A beginner's mind asks, "Now what?" and looks to the new opportunity for learning as just that—an opportunity. It includes being an astute observer of others and of the world around us. This level of attention and observation creates an opportunity for spontaneous learning.

Most of those interviewed indicated that paying attention to other people in similar situations was a very important way to gather relevant information. Among the various ways people acquire information directly from others are the following:

- Talking to people who seem to have knowledge and experience.

- Watching and observing those whom others think of as experts in the field.

- Observing everyone involved. Seeing how the experts and others work together, including the ways they act and interact and what they do with the information gained.

- Cultivating relationships with people who have expertise in the particular area of interest, or in areas that directly or indirectly impact the specific area of interest.

- Paying close attention to people who are in similar situations or who are pursuing similar interests—particularly noticing their mistakes.

- Developing cooperative relationships with others who have an interest in the area. Finding ways to work together and share information.

- Getting coaching from others who seem to be getting the job done or producing the kind of results you want to achieve.

Observing and working directly with other people is an extremely effective way to gather information about a subject. This way of gathering information also shows us the value of bringing a beginner's mind and taking it all in.

When you notice everything that happens and how those with more knowledge and experience deal with situations well and not so well, you store that information for future reference just the same as if you were reading a book, listening to a lecture, or building or creating something with your hands. Sometimes this way of learning is even more effective than traditional or more formal methods of education.

Seeing the Risks

There is another important by-product of observing others who have knowledge and expertise. When the goal is developing *20/20 Foresight*, observing others is one of the most effective ways to learn to identify the potential risks. Noticing where others make mistakes, identifying potential pitfalls, and looking for all the ways that things could go wrong are essential tools for becoming an expert in any area of interest.

In fact, for one participant, this was a key element of observing others. It seems that for this person, watching how others do something or how they approach situations was both an opportunity to see potential risks that might arise and a way to recognize the differences between the way one person deals with something and the way another handles it. Seeing the alternative approaches and watching how they turn out is a great learning tool.

In addition to observing how someone does what they do, paying attention to the different ways people deal with risks or handle challenging situations can be absolutely invaluable. Few of us have the opportunity to do this in the same way that one of our participants has experienced but his observation about what made the most difference can teach us a great deal about the value of watching and talking with others.

In the interview with Chris, a commercial pilot who spent several years as an Air Force pilot and Instructor Pilot, we talked about the value of briefing and debriefing. According to Chris, the briefing and debriefing process is one of the most valuable tools in developing proficiency and gaining information. In fact, the briefing and debriefing would often last much longer than the mission or the flight itself.

The purpose of these meetings was to review carefully every single aspect of the flight or the mission, to consider all the possible things that could go wrong and look at all the options available to deal with situations that might come up. In the meeting, the pilots also looked at the purpose of the mission and what actions might be necessary to fulfill those objectives. Pilots shared alternative approaches to handling potential risks and examined the value of each option and how to apply each one in a responsible and practical way. This allowed pilots to be on the lookout for potential problems, to identify the unusual very quickly, and to acquire an instinct for when to take certain risks and when to avoid potentially dangerous situations.

The briefing and debriefing sessions also included a comprehensive discussion of the reasons a particular action was either taken or avoided. This was done for each piece of the mission or the flight. Being clear about the reasons or justifications for a mission or for a particular way of going about it not only helped the pilots' preparation, but it gave them a particular perspective from which to view everything that happened during the mission. When the perspective was clear, split-second decisions were easier to make.

Briefing and debriefing are tools we can bring to many situations but they are particularly appropriate when we are developing proficiency in a new area of interest. The briefing and debriefing process does not have to be as long and drawn out as the sessions pilots go through, but it can help us be clear about what we are out to accomplish and then look to see what happened and how we might do it differently next time. The accomplished model train enthusiast doesn't just start laying track and hope for the best. There is usually a carefully drawn plan that is developed by using imagination, creativity, and knowledge. The same is true for the quilter who is designing art by sewing or the lawyer who is preparing for a mediation session.

Other tools identified by interviewees as great resources for gathering information on the road to proficiency included using the technical, investigatory, and puzzle solving skills that they already have in order to learn more.

Dave talked about how important it is that each one of us draws on everything we already know during the process of developing expertise—not because we know it but because it might be useful. This can be challenging because Dave is also the one who first mentioned bringing a beginner's mind to new areas of interest. However, the two are not as mutually exclusive as it might seem at first glance.

When someone is a beginner, there are few, if any, limits on what's possible. However, as we become more knowledgeable and develop expertise, one pitfall is that the things we see as possible are more limited. We start to look at what we are doing through filters that we acquired as we gathered information. These filters tell us what is possible, and we forget these are limits we are imposing on ourselves. In that moment, we are no longer automatically bringing a beginner's mind to the project. We now know something, and knowing something often stops us from being creative and inventive.

In addition to actively reminding ourselves to bring a beginner's mind to the subject, we can do more. We are very good at drawing on skills we think are related to the area we are learning, but we don't necessarily look to other skills or to knowledge about other subjects as a way to build skill or expertise in an area. It seems as though we first need to see that there is a logical link between the two areas before we start to apply our skills and knowledge in one area to the process of gathering information and developing expertise in a new area of interest.

For example, there seems to be no logical link between training as a bodyguard and recognizing the behavioral indicators that someone is a potential risk of harm to children. However, the observation skills that are essential to protecting someone you are guarding from harm are exactly the same observation skills that help us recognize adults in the environment who are a risk of harm to kids based on their behavior. The bodyguard can use these already finely tuned observation skills to identify the red flags that indicate someone is a potential child molester.

The two areas may, at first glance, seem unrelated. However, finely honed observation skills can make a big difference when one is learning something new and wants to develop *20/20 Foresight* in this new area. Part of bringing that beginner's mind to the subject is being willing to give up any preconceived notions of how it should go or how it should be and to see the potential in every opportunity, circumstance, or issue. When you add that to other skills and abilities that might increase the potential for learning, it can act as a booster to the process and propel everything forward.

As Dave said, one thing to remember is to use the skills we already have to enhance our ability to learn something new. We can learn a great deal more in a shorter period of time if we draw on everything we already know during the process of developing *20/20 Foresight* in this new area.

According to participants, gathering information also includes drawing on your own experience, particularly to identify past and potential problems. This requires being dedicated to breaking things down to the simplest level and making sure everything is clear. When we do that, we have a better chance of seeing the unusual and of always being on the lookout for new avenues of information. Gathering information means analyzing everything from the question: "What needs to be done here to be successful and how does this information help accomplish that?"

When the objective is to become an expert or to develop *20/20 Foresight*, ultimately the process demands that you seek out and ask for what you need and want, and you develop a craving for anything that can help you accomplish your goal of being proficient in this area of life.

CHAPTER SEVEN

Practice

Practice is something we all understand. We have been going to batting practice or listening to parents reminding us to practice the piano since we were very young. Teachers gave us pages and pages of the same kind of math problems so that we could "practice" working them out.

We may not always think about the different ways we use the word or the different things we mean by "practice." However, there are basically three ways that we "practice."

One practice is the kind that is most familiar to all of us. Practice, as it most commonly is used, describes a pattern of repetition designed to allow us to improve our ability to do something, to get good at something, or to learn something new. You probably practiced your multiplication tables as a child. You practice a new piece of music or you practice throwing or kicking a ball. In fact, the famous answer to the question "How do you get to Carnegie Hall?" is "Practice, practice, practice!" People of all ages practice things every day in their efforts to get better at doing something.

A second way to practice is to engage in the activity routinely—not necessarily for the purpose of getting better, but for the purpose of being proficient at it. An example of this type of practice would be to practice law or medicine or some other profession or craft. We work at many things in life as a practice.

The third way we practice is by carrying something out or taking the actions that fulfill something such as practicing your religion or practicing meditation. This type of practice is evident when we are observing something or carrying it into action. This observing or carrying something out is the fulfillment of the thing itself. There is nothing more to do and nowhere to get to when we are practicing meditation or a religious practice.

In developing *20/20 Foresight*, all three areas or types of practice are part of the process at different times. Regardless of the specific type of practice, there is a central theme that is evident in all three types of "practice." Whether practicing to get better, practicing to do the work of it, or practicing to carry out something in action, the central element is repetition. Among the things practice and repetition accomplish are the raising of our awareness about our surroundings and the reasons why things work and why they don't.

Practice allows for an in depth analysis of the process or information. It is practice that allows us to operate with a high degree of effectiveness and, as Diane said, it is what gives us a chance to think things through and try to identify the things that could go wrong.

It is repetition that characterizes this tool in the skill development toolbox. Through repetition, several things happen. First is that a certain ease with the subject matter develops. With practice, we go from being new and uncertain about an area of interest to gaining comfort with a subject and experiencing effortlessness in some aspects of it. Through that ease and comfort, some things become obvious. For example, patterns become recognizable. Noticing patterns helps us develop *20/20 Foresight* in a variety of ways.

One interviewee spoke about the value of pattern recognition in clarifying what he saw as "risk avoidance boundaries." According to John, he was introduced to the need to set these risk avoidance boundaries at an early age when he or his siblings did something that got them in trouble. Before they got in trouble, there was a certain level of risk that was acceptable. In that moment when Mom reacted badly, he knew there was a new line defining the amount of risk that was within acceptable limits. Once the new line was established, they knew going over and through that boundary was risking being in trouble with Mom.

Patterns help us see things about the process, as well as defining the process itself. They also help us analyze how something went compared to how it was planned or how it was intended to go. This is one of the ways that, over time, we develop the ability to define what I call the "the parameters of normal" in any given situation.

These parameters of normal are similar to John's risk avoidance boundaries. Actions that occur within these parameters occur to us as normal and do not cause alarm or concern. Practice, and the ability to recognize patterns as a result of the practice, forms the beginning of our ability to recognize boundaries and risk factors. Through practice, we see the patterns that point to the boundaries of risk and we also begin to see the places where these boundaries can be exploited and expanded.

Practice also brings a certain rigor to the process. Through practice and repetition we can, over time, develop automatic responses—as long as what we do is what one participant called "perfect practice"; that is, doing it repeatedly the same way or the correct way.

Perfect practice helps us develop the automatic responses that are one indication of attaining proficiency. They demonstrate that there are now aspects of this area of interest or the subject that we are passionate about that are a natural part of our thinking and acting. Noticing and responding is so much a part of you that it occurs automatically and does not require conscious thought. It is just like the moments when you swerve to avoid a car that is suddenly backing out of a driveway in front of you or do any of the other myriad of things that we do as an automatic response to a possible risk.

An easy analogy is to remember a time when you got a new job or moved to a new house. All of a sudden there was a new road between office and home and you started practicing it daily. Eventually it became your habit, and sometimes even when you plan to stop somewhere on the way home, you suddenly find yourself driving into the driveway. You automatically drove the route you always take and you did it almost mindlessly or without thinking. Driving home from work became automatic, and the only thing that interrupts that instinctive or, as some would say, programmed activity is if something that is outside the parameters of normal happens on the drive home.

Nancy, the corporate trainer, described a process she has developed as a direct result of applying rigor to practice. The process allows her to conduct training on any subject using materials developed by her company or the clients, and produce exceptional results every time.

When working with written material such as books, manuals, and articles, she begins by highlighting the key facts or key knowledge points. Then she drafts questions and answers that arise out of reviewing the material. The next step is to create a board display or a flip chart that highlights the important pieces of information. Then she organizes everything in methodical steps. Finally, she identifies ancillary things that the material points to and follows the same process with them. This process, which is now practiced and automatic for her, makes it possible for her to absorb new material really quickly so that she can give it to others. She describes herself as someone who can train others on any written material that she is given and who can train others to do so as well. For her, practice makes "practiced" and "practiced" is the same as reliable.

Practice and repetition are essential to developing *20/20 Foresight* not only because they allow us to develop a comfort and ease with the issue or process, but also, as three of the interviewees indicated, practice improves both our ability to react to circumstances and situations and the amount of time it takes to react. This particular tool is a pivotal part of the development of a high level of expertise. It is through practice—perfect practice—and repetition that the task or process becomes second nature to us. When that happens, we are able to begin to exploit the boundaries, take risks, and test new theories and processes. It is this tool that allows us to look for and identify the unusual and to develop and hone our ability to focus.

This practice and repetition also help us develop instincts that trigger a warning sign or red flag when subtle differences appear. Being able to identify the potential risks and take action to avert any number of problems is what ultimately defines whether we are truly proficient, truly skilled. Many people can learn to do something and do it well, but it is the practice that gives us a clear picture of risky places in a process and the potential threats that arise—in other words, practice, in all its forms, is essential to developing *20/20 Foresight*.

CHAPTER EIGHT

Paying Attention

Seems logical, doesn't it? Paying attention is an important part of developing *20/20 Foresight*. It is just simple common sense. Perhaps, however, it would be a good idea not to take it for granted that people pay attention. Each of the research participants said the need to pay attention, to be present, and to observe what's happening around them was a critical aspect of developing the level of skill that makes someone an expert and one of the most difficult to sustain.

Paying attention is not as easy as it sounds. Even if we start out paying attention, it is really very, very hard to keep it up. If you think about it, most of our time is spent anticipating what will happen next, rethinking what just happened, or deciding what we are going to say when the person we are listening to stops talking.

Paying attention means being alert and attentive to what is happening here and now. It includes really being present to what is happening in the moment. It means observing—consciously taking it all in. It is the experience we have on those somewhat rare occasions when our full attention is on what is happening, as it is happening. For many of us, this only occurs when we are facing a situation that creates either anxiety or excitement in the present moment. That these times often are linked with memorable moments or events reminds us that they are rare—that they are the exception rather than the norm. For example, we are fully present when we suddenly find ourselves driving on icy roads, or when our child takes that first step. We may be fully present when we pledge our love and life to another in marriage or watch a loved one accomplish a remarkable goal. For most of us, being present is measured in moments. However, being present or observing what's happening in the moment allows us to accomplish a great deal as we are developing *20/20 Foresight.*

First, it gives us an opportunity to get a clear, true picture of what's happening right now—and right now—and right now. In other words, when we are being present to what's happening around us, we are paying close attention to the details of what's going on, increasing our ability to begin to identify the boundaries of "normal" in the situation.

One of the participants, the pharmacist, Kathy, put it this way. She said if we know what's normal and are aware of what's happening, then referencing or measuring what's happening against the "normal" helps us see the warning signs that something is off or there is a risk on the horizon. When we are observing or paying attention to what is happening in the moment, we can see a lot of problems before they become a serious issue. When that happens, we often are able to take actions necessary to intervene before any damage is done.

To observe means to be aware of something, especially by paying careful, focused attention—to watch attentively or to notice.[xvii] Observing gives us an opportunity to process information through the filters created by the things we already know and the things that we have experienced in the past. When we do that, we begin to be able to establish realistic expectations and develop the range of parameters of what is considered normal in the situation.

Kathy also pointed out that observing heightens our awareness of our intuition about situations, circumstances, and people. We all have instincts that tell us something is not right. For the most part, we don't completely trust those instincts. Instead, we apply logic or some other reasoning process to the situation and discount our "gut feelings" about someone or something. When we are paying attention and being focused, those instincts become more pronounced and we are more likely to pay attention to them.

In addition, observation allows us, according to Diane, to review, revise, and further fine-tune our skills in a particular area. Diane pointed out that when we pay close attention, we can see how to improve something because the smallest thing begins to be noticed and attended to. When we pay close attention, we can improve our own skills and abilities dramatically.

According to JoAnn, paying attention also gives us a chance to see the whole of something rather than just the separate parts. Many people think close observation means only that we are concentrating on the pieces and parts of a situation. However, paying close attention also can allow us to see how it all fits together to create a whole picture. Seeing the whole picture also allows us to identify the potentially risky situations, circumstances, and issues.

Paying attention is not just about observing how things are going. It also means noticing and observing others—particularly when they make mistakes. In those times, we have the opportunity to learn and to recognize the subtle or slight differences that can open the door to a whole new approach to dealing with an issue or concern.

For those of us like Mary whose area of expertise includes direct communication and working with others, paying attention to and carefully observing what's going on with others is essential. A mediator must be able to listen for and identify signs that indicate how the conversation is going and how each party is responding in order to know whether the discussion is making any impact and when it is time to take a new direction. For example, she must notice whether the parties' facial expressions or body language are indicating any particular reaction to what the mediator is saying. The ability to observe and "size up" the situation must become, in Mary's words, "second nature" to a mediator—in other words, they must have *20/20 Foresight*. Paying attention is the access to being able to do that.

Paying attention also means using all your senses. We use our sight, hearing, sense of touch, sense of smell, and ability to taste to tell us what's happening and give us insight into what we know, and how we analyze what we think is actually happening in any given moment. It is through the five senses that we learn to recognize our passion, gather information, put it to use through practice, and observe.

What we learn and the skills we develop by paying attention and observing also teaches us something about how to be flexible, which is the next tool in the toolkit for developing *20/20 Foresight*.

CHAPTER NINE

Being Flexible

Someone who is flexible is believed to be responsive to change or adaptable—at least that is what the dictionary says.[xviii] Developing *20/20 Foresight* certainly requires flexibility.

Flexibility also means being willing to try something new and suffer the consequences, if there are any. It means being able to roll with the punches when something unexpected happens or when the situation calls for a new approach, a different perspective, or a revised plan.

When you realize that we develop *20/20 Foresight* in a dynamic or ever-changing environment, you can see that a willingness to be flexible is a crucial tool in becoming an expert in any area. As we learn from observation of others, we want to look outside the box for answers.

One of the things Dave shared was an aspect of this tool that has been particularly beneficial to him: as long as he remains flexible and does not get entrenched in a particular way that things should or need to go, he can continuously create and generate new ideas with no preconceived notions. When he is committed to being flexible, he keeps asking himself the question, "What needs to be done here to be successful?" In that situation, although he does not ignore his past experiences of what he already knows as he looks for the answer, he is not limited by past history in his efforts to find a solution.

Being flexible also is being willing to be surprised and excited as well as confounded or disappointed. This is possible if you recognize that most of the time, there is no "right" answer or "right" way to go about something. There are ways that are more successful, or easier, or perhaps even more productive, but being flexible means being willing to set aside doing something the way it has been done in the past in favor of an alternative approach or action.

One of the key elements of *20/20 Foresight* is the ability to distinguish and consistently recognize the warning signs that something is about to go wrong. Being flexible allows us to practice and pay attention while at the same time maintaining the ability to notice what's happening and to respond quickly and spontaneously to changes in the situation.

Flexibility is also about adaptability. It allows us to take in new circumstances and situations and deal with them in a way that limits the chaos or the destructive consequences. It also opens the door to new ideas. Flexibility encourages us to trust our instincts and helps us sharpen our ability to react to circumstances and warning signs that tell us something is not right.

Our ability to react automatically to situations that arise is what tells us we have *20/20 Foresight*. Being flexible, and applying that flexibility to circumstances that arise, is a key piece of the process that leads to achieving expertise.

CHAPTER TEN

Operating in the "Zone"

Lots of participants talked about operating in the "zone" but what does that mean? It is one of those concepts that are difficult to describe. Some might say the famous words of United States Supreme Court Justice Potter Steward in describing pornography might also apply to being "in the zone." In *Jacobellus vs. Ohio* Justice Steward said he could not define pornography but he knew it when he saw it. Most of us can apply that same standard to being "in the zone." We can't define the "zone," but we know when we are operating in that space.

The dictionary says that, in addition to describing a specific area designated for a defined purpose, zone is "a state of focused attention or energy so that one's performance is enhanced."[xix]

Books have been written about the subject and athletes are always looking for ways to get "in the zone" and stay there.[xx] The Mayo Clinic says that being in the zone is mental conditioning and there are four core techniques upon which this mental conditioning is based: relaxation, imagery, goal setting, and positive thinking.[xxi] Clinical & Sport Psychologist Dr. Ray Mulry, says that the four core competencies of "self-mastery" or being in the zone are: relaxation, balance, flexibility, and focus.[xxii]

For the participants in this research project, being "in the zone" was described in a variety of ways. To Marty, the physician who flew Cobra attack helicopters in Viet Nam, being in the zone occurred like being on autopilot. He was in the zone when reactions were automatic and warning signs of potential difficulties were triggering an appropriate response.

Kathy described the experience of being "in the zone" as being intuitive, and Brian agreed with both Kathy and Marty that the experience is not something that requires thoughtfulness or processing. It is automatic response action.

For Charles, being in the zone is something he called "practicing things out of existence." By that he meant practicing something long enough and well enough so it becomes automatic and requires no conscious thought or conscious action to engage. Both he and Mary acknowledged that these reactions and responses are those that now are second nature to them.

Shannon also pointed to the automatic nature of being in the zone. She likened it to a child instinctively developing survival skills.

Very small children begin to develop instinctive responses that assure survival. Tiny babies cry to alert their caregivers when they are hungry or need diapers changed. The child knows something is not right, and the automatic reaction is the one they discovered in the first moments after they came into this world. They cry!

Parents learn to respond to the cry, and eventually the parents can tell what the baby needs by the way the child is crying. So, when the baby cries a particular way, the parent responds accordingly. The baby sees that this works and over time, it becomes automatic. Some children never outgrow the concept that crying gets you what you want.

As babies, we begin with crying. As we grow older, we begin to identify the limits on the risks we are willing to take in life. Over time these limits form our boundaries and they become the flash point for our automatic reactions. We act instinctively to avoid harm or to protect ourselves.

As Jeff pointed out, many of these are so automatic that we are surprised at the way our body reacts and only notice it after the fact. Examples of this can be found all over our lives. The earlier example of driving home from work without realizing where you are until you arrive in your driveway is one we have all experienced. A comedian recently pointed out an example that most of us over 30 can relate to when he said that when he was growing up, there were no seatbelts installed in cars. The "strap" that crossed our bodies and held us safe when something happened in the car was our mother's arm. That, too, was an example of the automatic nature of an action when we are operating "in the zone."

Jeff shared an example of this automatic reaction when you are "in the zone" through an incident that occurred shortly before his interview for this project. He pointed out that although it had been several years since he had trained as or functioned as a bodyguard, he obviously learned at least one of the tools of that profession extremely well.

As a bodyguard, he was trained that when anyone approached him or his "principal" in any way that appeared to be threatening, his left arm went up as if to reach out to keep distance between him and the other person, and his right hand went automatically to the location on his right hip where his gun was holstered. When he was training to provide bodyguard services, he practiced this response so many times that it became second nature. However, even he was surprised to see the extent to which this was ingrained in his thinking and acting. Late one night several years after his time as a bodyguard, he was approaching his car in a dark parking lot when a man began coming toward him in a manner Jeff perceived as potentially threatening. Jeff said that when he looked down, he noticed his left hand was reaching out, and his right hand was on his right hip exactly where, years ago, a gun and holster rested. The gun has been gone for several years, but the reaction was still ingrained and automatic.

Jeff's reaction was automatic, reactive, and in the zone. When we are proficient in an area of our life, this "zoneness" is something we just experience; it is not something that we do. Our reactions to potential problems become as automatic as the actions in furtherance of the passion or interest we are pursuing.

Diane and JoAnn also described operating in the zone as being immersed in their actions. They noticed that during those times, they have their attention only on what is happening in the moment. Again, at those times, they are paying attention to what they are doing and thinking right then. They also noted that when they are totally involved in the activities—when they are in the zone—time seems to move faster.

In the zone there is an ease about what's happening. If and when challenges arise, all there is to do is deal with them as soon as they come up. When we are operating in the zone, it is easier to see the possible risks—the potential challenges or dangers—and to take actions to avert disaster or to avoid problems.

Once we are operating in the zone, we have achieved a level of expertise in the particular area. There is always room for growth and development, but the basic ability to perform the job or take the actions with a great deal of efficiency, skill, and ability indicates that we have applied these tools and acquired an expertise. The test for whether we are operating "in the zone" comes when we are faced with a potential risk or we see a potential hazard on the horizon, and we take steps to intervene before anything bad happens. When we are there, we have *20/20 Foresight* in that area of our life.

CHAPTER ELEVEN

So, what's the point of knowing this?

In an earlier chapter, we discussed the fact that most of the time, knowing something makes little or no difference. Knowing how to lose weight doesn't cause weight loss. Knowing the risks of smoking has not caused society to eliminate smoking from our environments. Knowing that regular health checkups can protect us from serious health issues arising does not compel every adult to follow a regimen that supports health. Knowing that these issues are serious and can cause us long-term, even permanent damage does not make us take action.

As a result, it is safe to assume that knowing that the six skills discussed in this book can be used to develop *20/20 Foresight* in any area of life will make no difference either. If all we do is read the material and find it interesting, or think about whether we agree or disagree with the concepts and ideas presented here there will be no real impact.

Perhaps readers will know more about how we learn and become proficient in certain areas of our life, but the knowledge will just become something else that we know about and can carry on a conversation about, but knowing will make no real difference. However, something else is now possible.

We can all identify things we really want to be good at or think we "should" be good at, so perhaps finding and using these tools to develop skills and abilities is a great idea – as ideas go. The real benefit, however, is that we don't have to wait for an area to "interest" us or compel us to take action in order to develop *20/20 Foresight* in that area. We can look at all sort of things that we think we "really want to be good at" or even things we need to do, or are required to do, or even things we can see are a good idea to do, and even though we are not instinctively, immediately passionate about it, we can apply the tools and develop *20/20 Foresight*. We can develop a compelling interest and move forward toward becoming proficient in a new area.

We can use the tools provided here to address family concerns, business or career skill development, or even serious societal issues. We can also begin to create and develop personal development or educational programs that are built with these tools in mind and that provide people with everything they need to develop *20/20 Foresight* in any area. We can even develop programs to help people discover how to use this information and knowledge to further their own interests and deal with matters that concern them.

The tools can then become the access to developing expertise in other areas that we think we *should* be more interested in or that we *want* to care more about. Knowing these tools and becoming proficient at applying them to areas in our own lives will allow us to take on new areas of interest and, where we have been unsuccessful in the past in our efforts to generate a sufficient interest in a particular area, provide us with the missing link between the idea or interest and actually developing *20/20 Foresight*.

For example, as a parent, it seems logical that becoming proficient in the ability to identify behavioral indicators in the actions of adults who interact with our children that tell us the person is a risk of harm to children would be a high priority. Every responsible adult wants to protect children from sexual predators – particularly parents. In fact, parents are the ones with the greatest interest in protecting their own children and, since even the most conservative and comprehensive research estimates that one out of 10 men in the United States and one out of five women are molested before they turn eighteen,[xxiii] the problem is at epidemic proportions. However the need to learn about this is not enough to inspire many of us to become experts. Parents assume that because they are attentive and careful with their children that this risk does not apply to them. The reality is that this is not an accurate assumption.

Furthermore, even the few programs that raise awareness about the nature and scope of the problem have not triggered a big demand from adults in the community for help in developing *20/20 Foresight* in this area. The unfortunate thing about this is that if adults have *20/20 Foresight* that allows them to recognize risky behaviors in other adults in the environment, they can intervene before abuse occurs. Everyone agrees interrupting this cycle of abuse is a good thing, but few are willing to do the work to develop *20/20 Foresight* and incorporate these warning signs into the background of our thinking. In the more than 20 years since these new programs of awareness and education about potentially risky adult behaviors have been part of the child sexual abuse prevention landscape, only those who developed a compelling interest or passion in the issue have taken the steps to become proficient – to develop *20/20 Foresight.*

Adults who have participated in prevention programs that raise awareness about the scope of the problem of child sexual abuse in society are surprised by what they hear and astounded at the scope of the problem. They are interested in putting a stop to it, but they think that one - three-to-four-hour presentation is all they need. After all, they were already doing everything they knew to do to keep their children safe – and they are responsible caring adults.

It is not that parents are not interested. In fact, people—parents and others—want to prevent child sexual abuse from happening to any child. Responsible, csaring adults agree that this kind of assault on a child is abhorrent and needs to be stopped. The problem is that many adults still think this is can't happen to their child. No matter how much knowledge they gain in an awareness session, they still think this is a problem in some other neighborhood and impacting some other children living in some other environment and that they would instinctively know if someone were a risk to their children.

We learned, through the work of implementing the *Protecting God's Children*™ program in the United States, that when people come to the session and see the program, they are profoundly impacted by the issues raised. We learned they begin to shift their attitude about the need for all adults to become proficient in being able to recognize the signs and symptoms of an adult whose behavior indicates he or she is a potential risk of harm to children or young people.

Some who saw the program were compelled to develop the skills needed to be successful in their objective to make children safer. They have applied the tools we have identified here and are becoming experts at recognizing risky behavior in the adults who interact with their children and they are learning how to intervene to interrupt any possible problems.

Most, however, now simply "know" about the problem. They attended the three-hour program session. They know that prevention is the responsibility of adults and they are interested in being part of the solution. However, they don't follow up and take advantage of the materials and experts available so they can develop *20/20 Foresight* in this area. This does not mean they won't be able to put their knowledge to good use. They will be more aware of certain risks and they will recognize some potentially dangerous situations that they might not have been aware of before. This alone will create safer environments for children. This improvement in their ability to keep children safe is only a fraction of what would be possible if each adult developed *20/20 Foresight* in this area.

This is just one example of how applying the tools and skills identified here can make a difference in the way that we deal with issues in our life. If we think about it, we can see that knowing we have these skills and knowing we can apply them to many different areas of life gives us the power to decide for ourselves what we will do and how much we will do to become experts in many areas of our lives.

However, identifying the tools is only the beginning. Unless we put them to use, there will be no impact. Putting the tools to use in areas of your life where you are interested in becoming skilled, and using them to deal with certain areas of life that are not going so well or where we consistently fail to achieve our desired goal or objective, is the real value of identifying and defining the skills.

Distinguishing, defining, understanding, and using the tools for developing *20/20 Foresight* provides you with the ability to locate what's missing when you falter on the way to fulfilling a goal. Rather than relating to yourself as someone who never quite gets it done completely, you can look objectively at the tools and the steps needed to achieve *20/20 Foresight* and see where you skipped a step, or failed to use the tool to its full potential.

Applying the tools to areas of life where it is in our best interest to develop *20/20 Foresight* will allow us to make new mistakes and find new answers to old questions. It will give us the ability to deal with the failures in our efforts from a completely different perspective. Rather than reinforcing some idea that we can't do anything right or that nothing really works, we will be able to see that we just skipped a step or failed to utilize a particular tool in our pursuit of expertise and proficiency in this area.

Look around your life and see how knowing and applying the tools can impact your daily living. Notice how many times you started something with enthusiasm and gusto and never quite got it finished. Notice how many times something caught your interest or piqued your curiosity and, just as you started to get interested in learning more about it, something distracted you and you soon forgot that you were intrigued by this new area of interest.

The implication for students is also profound. If a student is great at math but can't seem to write a clear sentence that expresses a whole thought, these tools can point the way to dealing with that situation by applying these tools to the problem. What would it be like if teachers could help students, particularly students who clearly are capable of learning the material and becoming proficient, to identify where the *20/20 Foresight* process got derailed? Then, all you need to do is identify the missing step and find a way to apply that piece of the process to the issue at hand. If you see that the process never had a real chance of succeeding because the math whiz has no interest in or passion about learning grammar, the question becomes one of finding a way to stimulate a compelling interest in the subject. In addition to giving the student a new chance at getting material that has always been just out of reach, there is no negative impact on the students' self-esteem. Students can see that they just skipped a step in the *20/20 Foresight* process rather than relating to themselves as stupid, irresponsible, or something equally disempowering.

Sometimes we may have a compelling interest but because we believe the interest is enough to keep us going or we are convinced we already know all we need to know, we don't gather all the information we need. Instead, we skip right to practicing. Because there is no real foundation established on which to build, we never really develop *20/20 Foresight.*

In the past, our commitment often was derailed when we hit a bump in the road or came up against a roadblock. We blamed ourselves and decided we were insufficient, or a disappointment, or some disempowering adjective. If we apply the tools and steps to those situations, it is possible to see what happened, to backtrack and fill in the missing information or put in the step we skipped.

Being able to identify when we have skipped a step and then putting it in can open the door to a whole range of possibilities for developing more areas where we operate at a level of expertise and skill that demonstrates we have *20/20 Foresight*. We can make New Year's resolutions and keep them. We can address things about ourselves or areas of our life that we realize need our attention, but that we have never been able to muster up the interest to give it our full attention. There is virtually no limit to the applicability of this process, if we learn to use the tools and follow the steps for developing *20/20 Foresight*.

We may not have thought about it before, but *20/20 Foresight* is something that we already practice in some areas of our life. We just never realized our accomplishments in those areas were the result of the application of a set of tools we already had to some steps that we already knew were needed. Applying these tools and taking these steps can make *20/20 Foresight* available to us in many other areas and can help us deal with potential risks and dangers quickly and with a new level of confidence.

CHAPTER TWELVE

Putting It All Together

So, you now know what *20/20 Foresight* is and how the concept developed. You know that developing *20/20 Foresight* requires application of these six steps:

1. A compelling interest or passion

2. Gather information

3. Practice, practice, practice

4. Pay attention and be present

5. Be flexible

6. Operate "in the zone"

But how can you actually put this into practice in your own life, to address an area that is of interest to you? What would it look like to put the steps together and use them as a plan for developing *20/20 Foresight* in an area of your life?

Take the case that you want to develop *20/20 Foresight* in your ability to manage your finances to prepare for retirement. Where do you begin and how do you use the steps in *Developing 20/20 Foresight* to accomplish your goal?

Start at the beginning. The first thing you need is a compelling interest or passion. Perhaps that's already present for you, but what if it's not? How do you generate the type of compelling interest that will have you follow through with the rest of the steps to develop an expertise in this area?

Perhaps attending an estate planning workshop will give you an opening to create a compelling interest. Maybe a talk with your parents or other retirees that you know who are still working, or have taken jobs as greeters for Wal-Mart or some other low-paying job to supplement Social Security income, will inspire you to get interested in developing a working retirement plan and becoming proficient in managing your resources for the best possible outcome. Whatever it takes, don't go forward until you are clear that a compelling interest or passion is operating in the background. Without it, you are doomed to failure.

Once you have a compelling interest to deal with your retirement, the next step is to gather information. There are formal and informal ways to gather information on this subject. There is a wide variety of books available in bookstores and libraries that include guidelines for how to calculate what is needed for retirement and then how to accumulate the resources that you need to enjoy that time of life.

There are seminars about estate planning, online resources, lawyers, accountants, certified financial planners who can provide one-on-one consultation, and many other resources for learning about planning for retirement. Public radio and several television channels provide programs that share investment advice and take questions from callers and viewers about their specific areas of need. Television shows are available 24 hours a day to let viewers know what's happening in the financial markets around the world.

You can create your own plan for gathering information using the tools you find most helpful. For example, if you are a reader, use the books, Internet bulletins and newsletters, and other written documents to build the core of your knowledge. If you learn best by taking information and processing and discussing it with others, read some of the material and make a habit of listening to or watching shows provide expert information or meet with a financial planner to address matters relevant to your specific situation. Make use of all the experts you can find. Check their credentials and use the information they provide in a way that best serves you.

Once you have sufficient information, begin creating a financial plan and putting it into practice. In the area of planning for retirement, practice requires that you keep taking actions even if you don't see immediate results. Practice, in this case, is doing the thing over and over and over. For example, make a decision that you will deposit a certain amount of money each month into an income-producing savings or retirement account. Then do it every month, without fail. Don't let anyone or anything interrupt the practice of setting aside that specific amount each month.

At the same time you are continuing the practice of setting aside money, you must pay attention to what's happening in the financial world that could impact your future. Pay attention, stay current on information, and know what is happening to your investments.

This also means you must be willing to be flexible. Paying attention may result in the realization that something that looked good at the outset is no longer a reliable investment. You must be willing to adjust your plan to deal with fluctuating financial circumstances. On the other hand, being flexible may simply mean being willing to make changes if they are warranted. The plan may work just the way it is designed. Being flexible requires you to be willing to make adjustments if they are necessary and not to be entrenched in doing it a particular way on a particular time table.

Ultimately, the habits you develop through practicing, paying attention, and being flexible will serve you well.

You will begin to operate in the zone, and ongoing observation of your financial future and the needs of retirement will become part of your daily routine. One example might be that you now listen to the evening news with a new view or pay attention to financial reports that you once ignored. You will start to automatically listen for the possibility that certain situations may create future financial problems or benefits. Operating in the zone, being present and paying attention will help you be able to take quick, decisive actions to interrupt any possible loss of income, take advantage of any potential windfall, protect your retirement funds, and continue to build for the future.

Applying the six steps of *Developing 20/20 Foresight* to an area of life provides the potential to develop a proficiency and, at the same time, removes many of the opportunities for us to criticize ourselves for not taking action, or to serve up a good heaping helping of recriminations and blame when we think we should be doing better. Use the six steps to accomplish your goals. You will save time and energy, and your chances of succeeding will increase greatly when you redirect your interests from self-blame to concentrated action.

We all have developed *20/20 Foresight* in certain areas of our life. Applying these steps gives us the tools and the ability to bring this level of proficiency to any area of life that is important to us. Use them well!

ABOUT THE AUTHOR

Sharon W. Doty is a widow, mother, and grandmother and native OKIE living in who recently moved to Atlanta, Georgia. Throughout her work life, Sharon has taken on many different roles, always looking for the pathway to making a difference. She is an effective speaker and accomplished trainer. As a lawyer, she acquired a reputation as an astute and effective litigator working for victims of crime and injustice. Sharon has been an active part of community organizations such as the March of Dimes, Youth Service Centers providing shelter for abused and neglected children, the Margaret Hudson School for Pregnant and Parenting Teens and the Child Abuse Network.

In addition, throughout her career, she has researched and written programs, conducted training in child sexual abuse prevention for thousands of people all across the U.S., and authored numerous articles dealing with raising awareness about child sexual abuse and training adults how to protect children from abusers.

Sharon is also an accomplished singer who has been performing for enthusiastic crowds for over 50 years. Her credits include classical, semi-classical and pop venues as well as many years of service as a church Music Director in various parishes in Oklahoma.

However, of all the things that Sharon has done and is doing, the role she most treasures is that of "Grammy" to the precious gifts that are her grandchildren. With eight amazing, gifted young people to love and a great grandchild on the way, the joy of being a grandparent just keeps expanding.

RESOURCES

[i] Although nearly 6.4 million vehicle crashes were reported to police in 2017, this represents a very small number of accidents when you consider that more than 3,212,000 miles were driven that year. https://cdan.nhtsa.gov/tsftables/tsfar.htm.

[ii] In fact, in 2017, only 34,247 people were killed in automobile accidents. https://cdan.nhtsa.gov/tsftables/tsfar.htm

[iii]https://cdan.nhtsa.gov/tsftables/tsfar.htm

[iv] Smoking is the leading cause of preventable death worldwide. More than 16 million people suffer from smoking related illness and 7 to 8 million people annually die from these illnesses. https://www.cdc.gov/tobacco/data_statistics/fact_sheets/fast_facts/index.htm.
 In 2017 the leading causes of death were Heart 647,457, Cancer 599,108, Accidents 169,936, Chronic Lower Respiratory Disease 160,201 and Stroke 146,383. https://www.cdc.gov/nchs/fastats/leading-causes-of-death.htm

[v] TNCRRG is an insurance company whose shareholders are comprised of Catholic dioceses and archdioceses in the United States and a risk pooling trust that represents over 1,500 Roman Catholic religious community and congregation locations nationwide, including hundreds of grad

and high schools and over two dozen colleges and universities, www.nationalcatholic.org.

vi *Charter for the Protection of Children and Young People*, ©2005 (Revised June 2018) United States Conference of Catholic Bishops, Inc.
"ARTICLE 12. Dioceses/eparchies are to maintain "safe environment" programs which the diocesan/eparchial bishop deems to be in accord with Catholic moral principles. They are to be conducted cooperatively with parents, civil authorities, educators, and community organizations to provide education and training for minors, parents, ministers, employees, volunteers, and others about ways to sustain and foster a safe environment for minors. Dioceses/eparchies are to make clear to clergy and all members of the community the standards of conduct for clergy and other persons with regard to their contact with minors."

vii Gardner, H., *Development of Education and the Mind: the selected works of Howard Gardner*, Routledge, 2005.

viii S. Whiteley, *Memletics Accelerated Learning Manual: Discover the High Performance Learning System that Improves Your Memory and Helps You Learn Faster* (Advanogy Publishing, 2003), 4; LEARNING-STYLE INVENTORY, LEARNING STYLES: A MULTIPLE INTELLIGENCES APPROACH, http://pss.uvm.edu/pss162/learning_styles.html.

ixhttps://www.cdc.gov/tobacco/data_statistics/fact_sheets/fast_facts/index.htm

xhttps://www.cdc.gov/tobacco/data_statistics/fact_sheets/adult_data/cig_smoking/index.htm

xi Id.

xii Episteme and Techne (Stanford Encyclopedia of Philosophy)

xiii https://www.roadscholar.org/ Road Scholar, is a not-for-profit organization providing extraordinary learning adventures for people 55 and over in the United States and 90 countries around the world.

xiv Suzuki, S., *Zen Mind, Beginner's Mind*, Weatherhill, *Ninth Printing*, 2005

xv Id. at 13-14.

xvi Id. at 14.

xvii COLLINS ENGLISH DICTIONARY - COMPLETE & UNABRIDGED 2012 DIGITAL EDITION © WILLIAM COLLINS SONS & CO. LTD. 1979, 1986 © HARPERCOLLINS PUBLISHERS 1998, 2000, 2003, 2005, 2006, 2007, 2009, 2012

xviii COLLINS ENGLISH DICTIONARY - COMPLETE & UNABRIDGED 2012 DIGITAL EDITION © WILLIAM COLLINS SONS & CO. LTD. 1979, 1986 © HARPERCOLLINS

PUBLISHERS 1998, 2000, 2003, 2005, 2006, 2007, 2009, 2012

xix COLLINS ENGLISH DICTIONARY - COMPLETE & UNABRIDGED 2012 DIGITAL EDITION © WILLIAM COLLINS SONS & CO. LTD. 1979, 1986 © HARPERCOLLINS PUBLISHERS 1998, 2000, 2003, 2005, 2006, 2007, 2009, 2012

xx Granat, J. P., *How to Get in the Zone and Stay in the Zone with Sport Psychology and Self-Hypnosis*, www.stayinthezone.com.

xxi Mayo Clinic Staff, *Mental conditioning: Is your brain in the game?*, May 2, 2006, http://www.mayoclinic.com/health/fitness/SM00001

xxii Mulry, R., *In the Zone*, Great River Books, September 1995, http://www.focusedbrain.com/inthezone.html.

xxiii Finkelhor, D., *Current Information on the Scope and Nature of Child Sexual Abuse*, 4 The Future of Children, SEXUAL ABUSE OF CHILDREN, No. 2, Summer/Fall 1994, 31-53.

www.ingramcontent.com/pod-product-compliance
Lightning Source LLC
Chambersburg PA
CBHW060516280326
41933CB00014B/2983